Attila by Laurence Binyon

A TRAGEDY IN FOUR ACTS

Robert Laurence Binyon, CH, was born on August 10th, 1869 in Lancaster in Lancashire, England to Quaker parents, Frederick Binyon and Mary Dockray.

He studied at St Paul's School, London before enrolling at Trinity College, Oxford, to read classics.

Binyon's first published work was Persephone in 1890. As a poet, his output was not prodigious and, in the main, the volumes he did publish were slim. But his reputation was of the highest order. When the Poet Laureate, Alfred Austin, died in 1913, Binyon was considered alongside Thomas Hardy and Rudyard Kipling for the post which was given to Robert Bridges.

Binyon played a pivotal role in helping to establish the modernist School of poetry and introduced imagist poets such as Ezra Pound, Richard Aldington and H.D. (Hilda Doolittle) to East Asian visual art and literature. Most of his career was spent at The British Museum where he produced many books particularly centering on the art of the Far East.

Moved and shaken by the onset of the World War I and its military tactics of young men slaughtered to hold or gain a few yards of shell-shocked mud Binyon wrote his seminal poem *For the Fallen*. It became an instant classic, turning moments of great loss into a National and human tribute.

After the war, he returned to the British Museum and wrote numerous books on art; especially on William Blake, Persian and Japanese art.

In 1931, his two volume Collected Poems appeared and in 1933, he retired from the British Museum.

Between 1933 and 1943, Binyon published his acclaimed translation of Dante's *Divine Comedy* in an English version of terza rima.

During the Second World War Binyon wrote another poetic masterpiece *'The Burning of the Leaves'*, about the London Blitz.

Robert Laurence Binyon died in Dunedin Nursing Home, Bath Road, Reading, on March 10th, 1943 after undergoing an operation.

Index of Contents
The Persons
Time
Place
ATTILA
ACT I
Scene I

ACT II
Scene I
Scene II
ACT III
Scene I
Scene II
ACT IV
Scene I
Laurence Binyon – A Short Biography
Laurence Binyon – A Concise Bibliography

The Persons

ATTILA, King of the Huns.
HERNAK, a boy, Attila's youngest son.
ONEGESIUS, a Greek, Attila's favourite counsellor.
SIGISMUND, a Burgundian, foster-brother of Ildico.
MESSALLA,   }
LAETUS,   } Roman Envoys
RORIK,   }
BURBA,   }Huns of Attila's bodyguard.
ESLA,   }
An Egyptian SOOTHSAYER
CHABAS, a Greek Refugee.
ARDARIC   } Subject Kings of the Goths and Gepids.
VALAMIR   }
ZERCON, a Moorish Dwarf.
HUNS, BURGUNDIANS, etc.
KERKA, Wife of Attila.
ILDICO, a Burgundian Princess.
CUNEGONDE, GISLA, and other women attendant on Ildico.

TIME: 453 a.d.

PLACE: A city of the Burgundians, conquered by Attila, in the valley of the Upper Danube.

ATTILA

ACT I

SCENE I

Part of a town of the Burgundians, occupied by **ATTILA**. A gate left, in a wall abutting on which, at the back, is the front of the house of **ILDICO**. At the right the colonnade of a large building, Attila's headquarters. Beyond it an open rampart.

Dawn. A comet in the sky, fading as the light increases. Within the colonnade **ESLA** and a group of armed **HUNS**; in the space beyond a few **MEN** and **WOMEN**, cloaked against the cold airy come and go, with terrified glances at the comet. **SIGISMUND** leans against one of the further pillars. **CHABAS** lurks in the background. On the rampart a stationary figure, the **SOOTHSAYER**, watches the sky.

Enter from the left **RORIK** and **BURBA**, with two other **HUNS**.

ESLA
All night it has so streamed, like a great torch
Blown by the wind.

BURBA
And now outglares the dawn.
Rorik, I like it not.

RORIK
Quake in your flesh!
It shall not fright me from my appetite.
These prodigies perturb a hungry soul.
Eat, eat and drink!

[The **HUNS** sit down to drink and dice, **CHABAS** comes forward, cringing.

CHABAS
Speak for me to the King,
Sirs! I have lent him moneys. I am lost.
The King forgets a poor man has his needs.

RORIK
Here 's pay for you!

[Strikes him.

BURBA
And usury too. Out, rat!

[**CHABAS**, driven off, goes toward **SIGISMUND**.

RORIK [Lifting his cup to the comet]
To Attila's splendor!

BURBA [Holding **RORIK'S** arm]
No, you drink our doom.

CHABAS
Ten talents! Listen, my lord Sigismund!

SIGISMUND [Turning his back]
Ten talents! Will that buy back liberty
For my lost land?

RORIK
Is that a mortal man
Or rooted effigy that stands and stares
On this dishevelled star?

BURBA
A man, but who
I know not.

ESLA
Tis the Egyptian.

BURBA
The Soothsayer?
The master of magicians?

ESLA
Half the night
He has watched this witch-fire burning, motionless.
Look now, he turns.

RORIK
Come, let us question him. —
O man of dreams and auguries, who read
Fate's crooked signs and characters, pronounce
This apparition's meaning.

HUNS
Ay, what means it?

BURBA
Famine, I fear.

RORIK
Some prodigy of luck.

ESLA
For Attila what means it? Good or ill?

SOOTHSAYER
Is not great Attila King over kings?

ESLA

But this hangs over Attila. Speak out.

SOOTHSAYER

You men of war, why seek to deal with powers
Who forge their ends behind the enacted scene?
Play your hot parts out; strike, slay and be slain!
To question blunts the sword, palsies the arm,
Curdles the blood: oppose her as you will.
Calamity will come

ALL

Calamity!

SOOTHSAYER

Hastes not for terror, tarries not for hope.

ONEGESIUS [Who has entered from the right during the last words]

Who talks of terror and calamity?
For whom?

SOOTHSAYER

For some.

ONEGESIUS

Ay, surely at this hour
The Roman streets throng with night-watchers pale,
Who cower and cry that this means Attila,
The terror and calamity of Rome.

HUNS

Hear Onegesius!

BURBA

Over us it hangs.

ESLA

Yes, over us, and over Attila.

ONEGESIUS

Fools! whom should Heaven give sign to but to him
Whom long ago it chose and certified
A meteor among men, a captain star.
The master of the warriors of the world?
Have you forgot the sword?

HUNS

Attila's sword!

ONEGESIUS
The miracle, the sword God flung from Heaven
There on the Scythian steppe: have you forgot
How when the Hunnish host stood in amaze
And terror as you stand now, Attila
Caught up the sword as 'twere God's thunderbolt
Of everlasting wrath? Have you forgot.
Who have seen it blaze in Attila's right hand
And armies quail before it? While the sword

ATTILA
Is with him, mortal cannot harm him. Now
This second sign, this glory out of night,
This plume, this flower, this fount of golden seed,
Attila takes to be his crest, a gift
From Heaven, a blazon of God's own device,
A brand to burn upon the battle's van
Lighting to victory.

RORIK
Ay, if battle came!
But Attila is changed; we rust in peace.

ESLA
How glib the Greek is!

BURBA
Now, Egyptian, speak.

SOOTHSAYER
Fear, fear: 'tis wiser.

ONEGESIUS
Still do you pretend
That Attila is menaced?

SOOTHSAYER
Attila
Himself may override the wave of doom.
I read not yet who shall be lost in it —
A man may own a dearer thing to wound
Than his own body. Attila has sons.

ONEGESIUS
This man talks treason. Seize him and keep close
In guard at the King's will. Away with him!

[Two **HUNS** arrest and take away the **SOOTHSAYER**.

There let the raven croak to the blank walls.
But you, I charge you, if your tongues report
Or private conversation entertain
This madness, 'tis at peril of your life.

RORIK
Spare threats, Sir Counsellor, you waste your words.
See, the thing's quenched, and the sun's up in heaven.

[**ONEGESIUS** parts the curtains of Ildico's house but is stopped on the threshold by **CUNEGONDE**.

CUNEGONDE
The Princess sleeps yet.

ONEGESIUS
Let her be awakened;
She is summoned by the King. I shall return.

[Exit **ONEGESIUS**. **CUNEGONDE** retires.

RORIK [Pointing to Ildico's house]
There is the portent you should look to, Huns!
No fiery mare's tail hung across the dark,
But one that wears a body, walks daylight,
A mischief with a woman's shape and eyes.
Plague strike and end all women!

[**BURBA** touches **RORIK** as **HERNAK** comes out, right.

Ah, my prince!
Now may my curse fall fortunate for him!

HERNAK
I have a new bow, Rorik,

RORIK
Let me try it.
A sweet note! But for those young arms 'tis tough.

HERNAK
Give it me back. See, I can bend it full.

RORIK
Come soon the day when I shall see your shaft
Dive to the feathers home in Roman flesh.

Are you for hunting? Shall I go with you?

HERNAK
I go alone. Rorik, tell not my mother,
For she forgets I grow to be a man,
And a King's son, whose word tall men obey.

RORIK
There speaks your father's spirit! Good hunting. Prince!
Be wary; the King's son is a great mark.
And discontented dogs of every tribe
Infest this place, to snap what gain they can.

HERNAK
I have my bow, my new bow, and sharp arrows.

BURBA
A Hun of the Huns!

RORIK
Why was he born the last?

CHABAS [Intercepting **HERNAK** as he is going out, left]
O my young lord, a boon before you go!
Speak favourably to the King for me.
I have waited month on month, and am not paid.
The King has many cares, and he forgets.

HERNAK
Speak to the Queen, my mother; she will hear.

CHABAS
My lord, I do beseech you!

HERNAK
Let me go!

[**HERNAK** shakes him off and goes out. **BURBA** and the other **HUNS** sit down to dice, **RORIK** paces up and down.

RORIK
Why was he not the first?
His brothers are but fit to follow him.
He captains them by nature.

ESLA
Ellak and Gengis,
Where are they gone?

RORIK

On foray, — quarrelling
As ever, which shall have the best of spoils.
Be it cattle or woman.

BURBA

Hernak for me! But come,
A hazard, Rorik.

RORIK

Pest upon all women!

BURBA

Why, what 's the matter?

RORIK

Witchcraft! Attila
Wavers, not strikes, stoops and not soars. And we,
That overstormed all Europe, Scythia, Thrace,
Sarmatia, Illyria, lands on lands
From Caucasus to Ocean, must we halt
Content as puddle-blooded citizens.
While Rome, that still defies us, is unwon?

ESLA

There 's thunder on the King's brow; when it breaks.

BURBA

Old Rome will tremble. Ay, he has deep thoughts. —
The luck 's all yours.

RORIK

'Tis witchcraft. Here we sit
With all the plains before us, cornered, cooped.
Stabled like oxen. O my soul is sick
Of being roofed and walled! Air! Bring a torch,
I say, and let these pale Burgundians burn
With the proud girl that rules them. Slaves to a woman!
That ever Attila cast eyes — O gods,
This should be the Alps, and yonder Italy,
Vines, towers clashing all their bells in fear,
Rich cities quaking, walls to leap, and Rome.

BURBA

The dice are dull toys.

ESLA

Hark to Rorik!

RORIK
Then
We rode like wind, we leapt like rattling hail;
Danube in flood-time could not race with us.
But now we must make platters of our shields.
And see our royal eagle witched and tamed,
A strutting pigeon in a castle-court
That coasts about the housetops and alights
To preen and coo. Lightning wither them all,
Pinch their lips cold, and mildew their soft cheeks.
All women, all, but specially this one.
This Ildico, who wastes our Attila!

ESLA
Is she the star with the long golden hair
That threatens all our heads?

BURBA
She has a bloom,
And there 's a fiery warning in her eye
Would tempt a man to tame her.

ESLA
They are proud,
These same Burgundians.

RORIK
I will find a way.

ESLA
Yonder 's her foster-brother, Sigismund,
Dogging her door; he too 's her slave.

BURBA
He 's pricked.
You have stirred him, Rorik.

RORIK
Were it not for her.
We should be feasting in imperial Rome.

SIGISMUND
Never will that be!

RORIK
Never! That 's a word

We know not. Will your lordship say us nay?

SIGISMUND
Remember Alaric.

RORIK
He sacked Rome.

SIGISMUND
And died.

RORIK
Alaric was not Attila.

SIGISMUND
Rome is Rome!
Your day is over, Huns; your King is staled
With conquest, he has lost the joy of it;
The terror of his end has come on him.
Three sons at odds, and you without a king;
Three sons at odds, and none to lead you. Laugh!
But you have seen the sign.

[Pointing to the sky.

BURBA [Starting up]
Stop the fool's mouth,
Or I will.

RORIK [Stopping him]
Not yet. I've a use for him.

SIGISMUND
You have seen the sign. Up, Huns, and save yourselves!
Seize what is yours. Attila scorns you. Up,
You are many! Wield a purpose of your own.
Let Attila beware then!

RORIK
I say too.
Let Attila beware.

ESLA
Look, the Queen comes!

[**KERKA** enters from the right,

CHABAS [throwing himself at **KERKA'S** feet]

Favour, O Queen, favour a wronged poor man
Who cannot reach the King's ear. Plead for me.
I ask no more than justice. Hear, I pray.

KERKA
Better thy fortune with the fortunate!

ESLA
Enough of whining, fellow; out of the way!

KERKA
Where is Prince Hernak? Have you seen my son?

BURBA
We saw him, — he was here some minutes since.

KERKA
I thank you. Is the King abroad?

RORIK
Not yet.

[She goes to the rampart and gazes out, then returns. The **HUNS** resume their dice.

CHABAS
That boy shall be my vengeance. The lion's cub
Shall pay me ransom.

[He goes out, left.

KERKA [Addressing the **HUNS**]
Am I not Queen among you? Did I not
Ride with you, hunger with you, thirst with you?
Do I lose honour, or are you Huns no more?
O that the wide plains were about us still
Of our own East! Then Huns were Huns indeed,
And Kerka wanted not for loyalty.

RORIK [Respectfully]
Mother of Hernak

KERKA
Thank you for that word!

RORIK
We suffer change, being mortal; there 's no help,
But we must bear the thing we cannot shun.

KERKA
Rorik, have Hernak in your care.

RORIK
I will.

[Exit **KERKA**.

BURBA
The setting sun!

ESLA
Rather the moon that hangs
Pale in the sunrise.

RORIK
Burba, here 's a thought.

BURBA
Let 's hear it.

RORIK
This Burgundian serves our turn.
With such a spur shall Attila be pricked.
I'll take this Frank, heap fuel on his flame.
Breathe discontent and wrongs so desperate
As stick at nothing; then, a midnight plot,
Swords out, and tumult! Attila once roused,
If we strike not the old fire from his soul,
Call me a fool.

BURBA
For a fight or for a feast
I am your man.

ESLA
And the Burgundian?

RORIK
Why,
We take him in the act. Kill, kill them all!
Come now, and drink to warlike days again!

[Exeunt all but **SIGISMUND**.

[**ILDICO** appears at the door of her house followed by **CUNEGONDE**.

SIGISMUND

Ildico!

ILDICO
Attila summons me.

SIGISMUND
Princess!

ILDICO
Speak then, but quickly.

SIGISMUND
The hour is come to act.
I have watched. I have planned. I have mingled with the Huns;
I know their thoughts. This streaming fire in heaven
Affrights them; they are muttering at their King,
Bated of prey and rapine. — Listen still.
I have men, I have swords.

ILDICO
See!

SIGISMUND [As **ONEGESIUS** enters, right]
Onegesius!

ONEGESIUS [To **ILDICO**]
The King commands your presence. He commands
That you this day, with all your women, quit
This house, and enter his house.

SIGISMUND
O shame! Shame!
Back to your tyrant!

ILDICO
Silence, Sigismund!
I speak, and for myself. — Sir, I refuse.

ONEGESIUS
That is your answer? Attila shall hear it.

[Exit, right.

SIGISMUND
Ah, now you understand him, Ildico!
The Hun must die. This comet beacons us
To the fulfilment of that fear it writes
Already on these savage hearts. Not ours

But Fate 's the deed. We want but Ildico
To lead us.

ILDICO
No more, Sigismund, of this.
Do I not know what it befits me do?
Stir not till I give word.

SIGISMUND
I wait the word.
Yet send it quickly. O, you cannot choose
But strike with us. Princess, my life is yours.
Fear not. If need be, I will strike alone.

[Exit.

ILDICO
O, put your arms about me, Cunegonde!
I want a friend.

CUNEGONDE
You have one.

ILDICO
I have you.

CUNEGONDE
And Sigismund.

ILDICO
Yes, Sigismund. But he
Would use me; and I 'll be no instrument
Of his or any man's. He plots and schemes.
Fool, fool, to match himself with Attila!

CUNEGONDE
Together, not divided, you were strong.

ILDICO
We were playmates together, girl and boy,
And dear remembrance knots our youth; but now
We are not children, playing harmless games.
But face to face with terrible men. I count
The cost, and know sweet ties may break; but this
Is chosen and determined. I will meet
This our great enemy.

CUNEGONDE

He never spares.
You have defied him; think what power is his!
O rather flee.

ILDICO
Whither?

CUNEGONDE
With Sigismund.

ILDICO
I'll counsel, Cunegonde, to a king's daughter!
Nothing is ever wise that is not brave.
All then were lost.

CUNEGONDE
But Attila — you know
That you have stirred his passion. If already
He has not snatched and taken you by force
And slain us all, it is that he will show
More surely now the savage Hun he is.

ILDICO
He has spared till now. You wrong him, Cunegonde.
Can one man rule a sea of raging men —
Have power to kindle them and calm at will —
By being brute as they are? Attila
Is greater than ten thousand of his Huns.
By his greatness, or his weakness, I will move him,
Pleading for all of us. Go, Cunegonde,
Seek Sigismund. Forbid him stir a hand
Till I command it. This must be. Go, now!

CUNEGONDE
And must I leave you? Will you stay alone
For Attila?

ILDICO
Alone. Fear not so much.
If I be driven to the uttermost,
If he should deem me like those Tartar women,
The only women of whose ways he knows,
Servile in blood and custom, that take pride
To be no more than a just-tasted cup,
A fortnight's fondling, a staled sweet, the last
Addition to his pleasure — if he think this,
Let me be accurst or he shall surely know
My difference. Sooner than a mouth of shame

He shall kiss death!

CUNEGONDE
What have you said? To kill
The master of the world! No man of all
The thousands hating him has lifted hand
To dare a thing so terrible.

ILDICO
Tis true.
When some divine and more than mortal deed
Is to be done, the strong, the wise forbear,
And when a greatness through weak heart and hand
Stammers into the splendour of a deed,
Pronounce it madness. — Go, seek Sigismund!

[Exit **CUNEGONDE**.

[**ATTILA** enters, right.

ATTILA
So; I am defied!
The word is yours.

ILDICO
Attila
A woman! Never man
Yet challenged Attila and lived: but now
A woman dares to brave him. — What are you?
A witch's incarnation, without use
Of bodily senses or the taste of pain?
No, flesh and blood, I swear! Bethink you then,
If I but lift a finger, you are crushed
Into what doom I choose. — Look in my face.
You are quailing in your heart,— confess to it.

ILDICO
What if I be? O, I can feel and fear.
No magic art defends me, no, nor hope
Of help; my flesh fears, but not yet my soul.
Put chains upon my body. Do all your will.
I am not, shall not, cannot be your slave.

ATTILA
So proud?

ILDICO
What would you have of me? Hate, hate?

Such an immortal hate

ATTILA
Have I struck fire?
Flame, then! A woman's hate — I never knew
A woman kindle

ILDICO
No, you never knew
A woman not a slave; but we, but we
Women of the West are of another mould.
You smite in me a people.

ATTILA
Conquered!

ILDICO
No,
You tread on fire.

ATTILA
My heel can stamp it out.

ILDICO
But it will smoulder till it burst afresh.

ATTILA
What 's this? What do you speak of? Tell me more.
What seek you of me?

ILDICO
Attila's glory! O,
Listen! Within these sheltering walls a child,
That from these towers eyed often the vast plains,
The hills, and Danube rushing to the East,
Grew up; and, ere she was a woman, heard
The rumour of the name of Attila
Come rolling like a thunder from afar.
She pictured him most royal; she was born
Of generous free blood; she saw him stride
A demi-god, a god, a destiny.
That plucked up kings like thistles: cities burned
To be his torches; he was born to exceed
All measures of men's thought. — She was a child.
But now—

ATTILA
But now?

ILDICO
She is a woman now,
And she has known what madness in men's blood
Binds them like hunger; tasted the sharp breath
Of suffering, and beheld the different world
Dark under cold heavens, deaf to anguished cries
That pierced into her heart. And yet sometimes
She listens to her old thoughts asking her
Will Attila be less than she had dreamed?
Will he, even he, be nothing but the storm
That yesterday crashed on our roofs, and now
Where is it? None knows. O, you burn and waste;
But blackened earth teems richer for her loss
When all your Huns are past. — Speak, Attila!
I have told my heart out, I am in your hand.
Take me, and bind me, and kill me — what you will —
But let my people free! I plead for them,
As I will answer for them.

ATTILA [After a pause]
You are free.

[Then with passion.

Ildico! —

[**ILDICO** has disappeared into her house without looking back.

[**ONEGESIUS** enters, right.

ONEGESIUS
Is she humbled as befits?

ATTILA
She is humbled as the hawk is when he mounts,
Or lioness that's hunted from her mate;
A mother-mould of stormy-hearted men!

ONEGESIUS
Better to take and to forget her, King.

ATTILA
I'll have her soul, not only her body, mine;
And surely as the heart beats at my ribs
Mine shall she be. To touch resistance, feel
Within my fingers the proud, delicate flower.
And not to harm what I could crush at will

In an instant — there 's an edge and zest in this
Those women of the East, of my own race.
Never provoked. But I shall tame her. Well?

ONEGESIUS
This soothsayer

ATTILA
I have heard an oracle
Speak from a woman. Onegesius, what say you?
Shall the Hun plant his spear in the old earth
And strike a root, to branch abroad, and end
His wanderings?

ONEGESIUS
The Hun's blood can never rest.

ATTILA
Rome mocks me, mocks me with her thousand years.
My spear should be the king-post of a house
Deep-founded and enduring.

ONEGESIUS
This soothsayer,

ATTILA
What mischief has he told?

ONEGESIUS
Your soldiers fear
That nightly portent streaming past the stars.
And this man threatens.

ATTILA
Me? God's sword is mine.

ONEGESIUS
'Tis not yourself he hints of peril to.

ATTILA
What then?

ONEGESIUS
Your line

ATTILA
My line?

ONEGESIUS
Your sons.

ATTILA
My sons!
I'll see him! Were that true? Now I remember
'Twas prophesied before. At Danube's passage
A witch croaked thus. I'll see this soothsayer.
Bid him prepare: furnish him all his art
Has need of: he shall question Fate. My sons!
I must have sons; I am maimed without a son.
I melt and crumble like the summer ice
With all my empire, if I have no son;
But I will be eternal as this Rome,
So I have sons.

ONEGESIUS
When shall the man await your majesty?

ATTILA
Fear knocks upon my heart, lest this be true.
— To-night, to-night!

ONEGESIUS
Shall the Egyptian die?
Silence is safest.

ATTILA
No, I fear him not.
Whatever secret the locked lips of Fate
Yield to his art, be it good or ill, I'll know it

[Exit **ONEGESIUS**.

Dust! to be ended and extinguished here
In my own body! All of me that goes
Riding to conquer Time, lost, overthrown!
And Rome remaining, Rome remaining!

[**HERNAK** enters, left.

HERNAK
Father!

ATTILA
There's blood upon you, boy!

HERNAK

Father!

ATTILA
Blood!
Does it begin already? — You are pale, you tremble.
Where are your brothers? Is there news of them?
You are hurt, boy. Speak 1

HERNAK
I am not trembling, father.
'Tis not my blood. I killed him!

ATTILA
Tell me again.
— Could Chance, could Fate in fleshly form appear.
That were a thing to kill.

HERNAK
I am your son.
I killed him; he is dead.

ATTILA
Who dead? How dead? Was there no stroke from Heaven?

HERNAK
It was a Greek who supplicated me
When I was going out; I would not hear,
And he came after me, and in the hollow
Down by the postern met me suddenly.
He had a horse and caught me to his saddle,
Swearing you should pay ransom for your son.
And spurred away. But I was not afraid.

ATTILA
No, Hernak.

HERNAK
And my knife was in my belt.
I caught him by the throat and stabbed him.

ATTILA
How?

HERNAK
The Hun's way, so!

ATTILA [Kissing him]
Brave Hernak! That 's my boy!

HERNAK
I am a man now, father, am I not?
I would be like my father and hear men say
'He is Attila's own son.'

ATTILA [Putting him away]
More terrible
Than Attila, I hoped . . .
[With sudden suspicion.]
Where is your mother?
Speak, boy!

HERNAK
What changes and what angers you?
Why do I vex you?

ATTILA
Did she set you on,
Smeared with false blood and tricked with a false tale.
To play upon the father's pride in me?

HERNAK
I told the truth. You never taught me lies.

ATTILA
Go wash that blood off.

[**HERNAK** withdraws.

Whence fell that shadow? Tis but shadow, yet
How strangely colours as in fatal hues
What is mere accident! The boy 's unhurt.
Why should Fate play these tricks, make mouths at me
Behind a horrible mask, to snatch it off
And smile — and smile!
[With sudden change]
Hernak! Son! My son!

HERNAK [Running back]
My Father!

ATTILA
We 're not taken, spite of Fate
And all her gins; we 'll make her omens laugh.
You and I, boy. You shall surpass me yet,
And we will war down everlasting Rome—
The weak can never wait, but I am patience —

Your son's son shall inhabit Caesar's house.
The ships on all the seas shall be his ships:
Far into Time I see them . . . sons! My sons!

CURTAIN

SCENE I

A vaulted room. A door at the back left, another small one at the rights near which the **SOOTHSAYER** stands with eyes fixed on a small stone altar on which aflame bums.

ATTILA enters, followed by **ONEGESIUS**.

ATTILA
What has the fierce star written? What is hid
In heaven against me? Tell me of my sons. —
Onegesius, leave us. Wait without the door.

[**ONEGESIUS** goes out, closing the door.

[To the **SOOTHSAYER** after a silence.

Thou art in my hand!

SOOTHSAYER
And thou, O Attila? . . .

ATTILA
Find me the means to satisfy my soul!
If holy or unholy arts have power,
If by persuasion or by force thou canst
Ravish from Time his secret, drag it forth! —
I hear you famed beyond the common tribe
Of soothsayers; magicians call you master.
Prove it! Whence got you this so potent lore?

SOOTHSAYER
Chaldean sages taught me in their towers
That watch the stars; in Egypt I was born;
Their art is patient to conjure and charm
Out of their time the face of hours unborn.

ATTILA
Summon them up.

SOOTHSAYER
What I can do, I shall.
But boast not more.
Behold, we walk our little hour of light
Toward this great dark that fronts us like a wall.
All we shall do is there, and all we fear.

ATTILA
Thrust and break in: seize Fate and force her speak.

SOOTHSAYER
Beware lest from her ambush, ere thou knowest,
She leap out at thee.

ATTILA
What 's the peril? Where?

SOOTHSAYER
Thou art threatened.

ATTILA
Ah!

SOOTHSAYER
This meteor that makes pale
The natural lights of heaven

ATTILA
Speak! What of this?

SOOTHSAYER
O Attila, a power stands over thee
Poising, but whether to strike out thy doom
Or to enrich thee, hangs uncertain yet.
The time awaits thy grapple; thou shalt know
When Fate makes of thy hands her implements
And thou the accomplice bring her deed to birth.

ATTILA
What power is this whose menace I must fear?

SOOTHSAYER
If my ancestral art have rightly spelled,
A woman.

ATTILA
Of my race?

SOOTHSAYER
Nay, strange to thee.

ATTILA
Her name?

SOOTHSAYER
Sign tells not: this is not revealed.
Yet of her blood she is born thine enemy.

ATTILA
Enemy born, yet may be turned to boon

SOOTHSAYER
Her destiny and thine are interlocked.

ATTILA
And nothing of the event?

SOOTHSAYER
I read no more.

ATTILA
Is this thy boasted art and magic skill?
Thou bat, thou owl, that chatterest in the dark
What every eye but thine sees plain by day!
Thou keep'st the secret back.

SOOTHSAYER
Patience, O King.

ATTILA
Bethink thee of some engine to extort
Fate's meaning, or I swear

SOOTHSAYER
Patience, O King!
Thyself must question; thou art in the plot.
The agent and conniving will: to thee
Fate will speak clear what is to others dark.
My office is to show thee how.

ATTILA
Begin!

SOOTHSAYER
All is prepared. Behold this altar-stone

ATTILA

What is the flame that burns so still on it?

SOOTHSAYER

Thy destiny! — Take in thy hand this dust
Compounded of all secret roots that mean
All manner of untimeliness to man.
Plucked at conjunction of disastrous stars,
And sprinkle it upon the fire.

ATTILA

What then?

SOOTHSAYER

If destiny, which is the flame, be bright,
'Twill be consumed, the fire will feed on it;
But if the doom be short, the flame will die.

ATTILA

So.

SOOTHSAYER

Seek thy fate then.

ATTILA

My fate? What of that?
My doom is dated somewhere in the book.
But I am girded with the sword of God
Which is the fate, part of whose will I am;
No, but the after-days and after-doom.
My empire and succession's heritage —
This troubles me: a wild witch long ago
Predicted me misfortune in my sons.
I would learn their fate.

SOOTHSAYER

Nothing of thine own?

ATTILA

Do as I bid thee!

SOOTHSAYER

Sprinkle then the dust.
Pronounce thy sons' names each in turn, and hold
His image in thy heart, nought else, the while.

ATTILA [Taking the dust in his hand]

This then for thee, Ellak, my eldest born!
The first that called me father — this for thee!
Thy mother bore thee on the Tartar plain.
Ah, wild and headstrong then I rode and fought,
Not yet a king, and wild and headstrong thou.
Ambition went not to thy getting, boy!
I would not have thee rule, save in such sort
As now, some subject tribe; thou art a hand
But not a brain — Yet, this for thee.

[He casts the dust on the flame, which goes out at once.

So sudden?
A straw would have burnt longer.

SOOTHSAYER
Fate so wills.

[He rekindles the flame.

ATTILA [Taking another handful of dust]
Gengis, my second, this for thee. Is thine
As short a date? Thou hast a subtle brain
And goest about with eyes upon the ground,
Getting thy ends; but no, thou art not loved.
Destiny will not choose thee.

[He casts the dust again, with the same result.

Gone! thou too.
Drive me to the outpost, I am not subdued;
But one remains, but one, yet he the best.
My Hernak! Fortune! if thou choose not him.
If thou use not this precious-metalled ore
To mould and to refine thy masterpiece.
But blindly waste it, then I 'll call thee all
That men have cursed thee for, convict indeed
Thy crooked and capricious purposes
In their proclaimed futility. Why then,
The world were chaos, Destiny no more
Than a giant idiot with a random hand
Stumbling and striking. 'Tis impossible!

[He is about to cast the dust, then hesitates.

If it should be? Hernak, my Hernak, brave.
Wise past his years, courteous, contained, beloved.
Flesh of my flesh, will of my will — all prayers

I ever prayed are in this hand!

[He casts the dust on the flame, which leaps a moment then goes out.

[To the **SOOTHSAYER**] Tis false.
Thou vile pretender! Thou hast been suborned.
Confess! I'll tear the life out of thy limbs,
Cut shrieking into pieces! I'll have all
Thy tribe of sorcerers suddenly put out
As these brief fires!

SOOTHSAYER
Perform thy threats; 'tis vain:
The Gods bear witness.

ATTILA
Tush! — 'tis true, 'tis true.

[He begins to pace up and down.

The badge of blood -was on him for a sign,
And I would not believe! My boy, my boy!
I thought to shoot an arrow fast and far:
It falls before my feet. . . .
When he was sucking at his mother's breast
My hope was big in him; but now — but now —
Must I be balked of all my soul begot?
I stamp upon the ground, and armies spring.
Thou shalt not have him. Death, or if thou dost.
By all the fiends and furies that rush in
To make their hell-home in the heart of man,
I swear that for each pang I suffer now
I will exact a thousand from the world,
I will spare nothing: Italy shall be
My vineyard, and the wine of it be blood —
Red spirting blood beneath my dancers' feet;
And Rome, Rome, Rome, out of her orphaned mouths,
Out of the cinders of her burning streets
Feast me with curses! Did I dream of peace?
'Tis blown to air. I 'll fix me on no throne,
But harry, scourge, be vengeance, storm, and plague;
And I will laugh as Fate now laughs at me,
Robbed of my lion's whelp.

[Turning suddenly on the **SOOTHSAYER**.

Get hence before I slay thee, mouth of evil!
Thy work is done, my work begins!

SOOTHSAYER
O King,
Remember yet the woman!

[Exit, left.

ATTILA
Ildico,
Ildico, Ildico? You gods! is this
Your meaning? Is her beauty the fell star
That strikes and blasts my sons? The sacrifice?
Now terrible and clear the omens read.
'Tis so, 'tis she. It must be. — Fate is Fate,
But Attila is Attila. So be it.
Let all behind be tossed into the waste.
My agony with it, all former hope
Razed out, life springs, life shoots and bursts anew!
She should bear royal children.

[**KERKA** enters hurriedly and throws herself at his feet.

Kerka!

KERKA
Woe,
Woe to our house!

ATTILA
Speak!

KERKA
Our two elder sons!
News comes that on a foray quarrelling—

ATTILA
You talk of ghosts that wander the wild air!

KERKA
They are dead? You know it?

ATTILA
Dead!

KERKA
If it be true
That miserably they have slain each other,
Still we have Hernak.

ATTILA
We?

KERKA
O Attila,
Thank we the Gods still for our best-beloved!

ATTILA
Ha, ha!

KERKA
Why do you laugh so dreadfully?

ATTILA
The hounds are yelping at the quarry's heel;
Their fangs grin; Death hallooes. The boy is down.
Gather your wailing-women, make the grave!
He is dead!

KERKA
He lives!

ATTILA
A moment, and no more.

KERKA
You rave! Remember how you prayed for him, —
The youngest, yet you swore he was the best.
Since on your knee he sat and with small hand
Drew your great sword a little from its sheath.
And looked into your eyes.

ATTILA
No more of that!
Out, grief, out of my bosom! Say no more.
I have put this all behind me.

KERKA
Attila!

ATTILA
The oracle has doomed him.

KERKA
It is false!
If it were true, my heart would know it first.
The heart beneath the breast that suckled him. —

Will you not use one fond word to your wife
That bore him you?

ATTILA
I loved you.

KERKA
Loved, loved, loved!
O bitterest of words to her that loves!

ATTILA
You should have borne another. It is too late.
Better to have been barren from the first
Than breed such hope, to blast it in the flower.
A malediction lies upon that womb!

KERKA
Ah! it is Ildico, not me, you love.

ATTILA
I say, that you are wife of mine no more.

KERKA
She! she! Yet Hernak lives. I know he lives!

[After a pause.

I am my lord's. I must bow even to this.
Heaven is just, Heaven will hearken. In that day
Remember me. You love out of your race.
Out of your blood. Think you that Ildico
Will be as Kerka? She will love, may be.
But with exactions, with suspicions, proud
In contraries to try you; something always,
As Western women in their nature use.
You 'll not possess, some citadel apart;
She 'll never give you of her very soul
As I you cast away.

ATTILA
Farewell.

KERKA
My sons!

[**KERKA** goes out as **ONEGESIUS** enters.

ONEGESIUS

What said the Egyptian? Ellak, Gengis slain?
What of the oracle?

ATTILA
Sponge out the dead!
The wound is here, but the hot iron put to it.
From now my soul despises to be hurt.
Fate strikes me to enrich me, stings to spur,
To stubborn and enkindle. I am chosen.
Destined.

ONEGESIUS
What mean you?

ATTILA
Attila is awakened.
And he will match him with this mighty Rome
That boasts her birth beyond the count of time.

ONEGESIUS
If it please you, hear—

ATTILA
I, I will be eternal;
Out of the teeming chaos that's to be
My will shall fetch and mould to form and flesh
Its long-unborn fulfilment: I have seen
In vision rising up a line of kings,
And each more terrible than the last.

ONEGESIUS
The present—

ATTILA
No counsel, Onegesius.

ONEGESIUS
Who should be
Mightier than Attila?

ATTILA
He shall come, I tell you,
And Ildico shall mother him.

ONEGESIUS
Beseech you.
Beware of Ildico, beware of her.
These same Burgundians are a sullen folk.

That cherish wrongs like oaths and sacred vows.
This marriage is unholy in their eyes.
Your death is dearer than their lives to them.
Take heed, lest perfidy stab home at you.

ATTILA
Pish! Gnats of summer, let them bite their fill.
What hour is it?

ONEGESIUS
Past midnight; dawn draws near.

ATTILA
Get you to bed. I shall not sleep.

[**ONEGESIUS** is going out; then returns.

ONEGESIUS
My lord.

ATTILA
What now?

ONEGESIUS
The Egyptian sorcerer. 'Twere well
That he were silenced. I fear blabbing tongues.
This man 's a danger.

ATTILA
End him as you will.
I have used him. Let all go that served my past.
The world arises new, and I with it.
— What was that noise?

ONEGESIUS [Listening at the door]
Some stirring in the town,
Far off. All 's still now.

ATTILA
So the future stirs.
To bed! I'll see the dawn up, Time's new dawn.

SCENE II

The same scene as in Act I. Night, **RORIK**, **BURBA**, and other **HUNS** gather near the gate.

BURBA
What of the King?

RORIK
I wait for Esla's word.

BURBA
Is it past midnight?

RORIK
The first cock has crowed.

BURBA
Give us our cues again.

RORIK
Stand to your stations:
You, Burba, there; I by the doorpost here,
The rest behind. No noise until the signal.

BURBA
Three knocks upon the gate, and on the third
We drop the bolt.

[Enter **ESLA** hurriedly.

RORIK
What now?

ESLA
A curse is on us.
The King is not abed, cannot be found.
He is gone with Onegesius, none knows where.

RORIK
That crafty Greek is ever crossing me.

BURBA
What 's to be done?

ESLA
They whisper that he tries
The oracles of that Egyptian.

RORIK
O,
We'll find him matter for his auguries.
This shall be richer sport. He shall be roused,

Fear not; I'll parley with this Sigismund,
Say Attila is warned, the secret known,
He must hammer on the door and come, swords out.
For open fight.

ESLA
Well thought.

BURBA
My fingers itch.

RORIK
Soft! not so loud. Already I have primed
A score of men to hold the several gates
And at the signal make such clamouring show
The town shall seem invaded and at arms.
Meanwhile we keep these Franks in noisy fence
Till the King comes; and when the hubbub grows
So huge a roaring as would start the dead,
And Attila with anger in his eyes
Strides in, why then — let swords leap all about him;
We'll spice his nostril with the scent of war,
Cry 'Kill!' and 'Lead us!'

BURBA
There 'll be slaying then!

ESLA
A merry time!

RORIK
Hush, all!

BURBA
Is it yet the hour?

RORIK
Some minutes still: wait for the knocking; now
Like mouse to hole.

[The **HUNS** retire to their hiding-places. After a brief pause **ILDICO** comes out from her house and sits down on the steps, her head in her hands, **CUNEGONDE** follows her and touches her on the shoulder.

CUNEGONDE
Here in the cold air?

ILDICO
O, I could not sleep.

I stifled. Will it soon be dawn?

CUNEGONDE
Quite soon.
Come, — come to bed.

ILDICO
What do you listen for?

CUNEGONDE
I thought there was a sound without the gate.

ILDICO
You tremble.

[Seizing her arm.

CUNEGONDE
Come away!

ILDICO
What do you fear?
What do your eyes seek yonder in the dark?
No, I 'll not come till you have answered me.

CUNEGONDE
It is not fear, but hope. Yet I fear too.
Sigismund — hark! — Sigismund is in arms.
He has mustered all the boldest of our folk,
And strikes to-night for freedom and for you.

ILDICO
My word was pledged he stirred not. Cunegonde,
Did you not carry my command to him?

CUNEGONDE
He is a man: he would not listen. Ah!
He is in peril; would you thwart him now?

ILDICO
Woe to you! You have betrayed me! You, my friend.
Where is the King?

CUNEGONDE
He sleeps.

ILDICO
What was that sound?

CUNEGONDE
A sword striking the wall.

ILDICO
The King, the King!
He must be warned.

ESLA
Back! no one enters here.

[**ILDICO** and **CUNEGONDE** retire behind the colonnade. Three knocks sound upon the gate.

RORIK [Coming forward]
Knock louder, man! Louder! The King is warned!
No use for secrecy. Make show as if
An army came. Hammer, to fetch him up!
A loud alarm! Then we shall take him here
Trapped and alone.

SIGISMUND [Without]
Open!

RORIK
Let fall the bolt.

SIGISMUND [Rushing in with a **TROOP** of Burgundians]
Attila, Attila! Where hides the Hun?

RORIK
He comes.

BURBA
Meanwhile a bout of fencing, friend.

RORIK
Lights, Esla, lights!

[**HUNS** bring torches.

SIGISMUND [Defending himself]
What devilry is this?

BURBA
Stand to your guard! Now were we not at play,
Your head were cloven through.

SIGISMUND

Where hides your King?
Let fall your blade a breathing-space.

BURBA
Good sport!

[An uproar without begins and increases.

RORIK
Now we will rouse him. Huns, he shall see blood!

[He kills a **BURGUNDIAN**.

BURGUNDIANS
Flee! Treachery!

[Some flee, pursued by the **HUNS**, who try to shut the gate.

HUNS
Kill, kill! Attila!

SIGISMUND [Still defending himself]
Snake, devil!
Was this your trap?

RORIK
For simple souls like you
Such traps are made. Stay, Burba, hold him yet.
And he shall have his stroke at Attila.

[**ILDICO** comes out among them.

ILDICO [To **RORIK**]
Free this man!

SIGISMUND
Ildico!

RORIK
At whose command?

SIGISMUND
Not that name, Ildico.

ILDICO
In Attila, the King's name, I command.

ATTILA [Suddenly appearing from the right]

Who speaks for Attila?

ILDICO
Ildico, my lord.
I am shamed. I knew not of this thing. I thought
My people heeded my command, — and yet,
Give me this man's life.

RORIK
Let me kill the slave.
He meant your murder.

ATTILA
Free him! By God's wrath.
Do you know your King?

[The **HUNS** release **SIGISMUND**, but disarm him first.

Your blades are ready; come,
I'll stop this hubbub. Burba, take your guard,
Speed to the north gate, put the riot down.
Rorik, with me!

RORIK
To the world's end, my King!
Now Attila is Attila again.

[**ATTILA** and the **HUNS** disperse right and left.

SIGISMUND
I had him in my hand. A thousand curses!

ILDICO
He shone like fire. O, this was Attila!

SIGISMUND
The traitor, the damned snake! And O, fool me!

ILDICO
Hark how the uproar at his coming dies.

SIGISMUND
Ildico!

ILDICO
Hark!

SIGISMUND

Ildico! Have you drunk
Of poison, are you witched with sorceries.
Is your blood changed, to have used that hateful name?

ILDICO
He set you free.

SIGISMUND
Ay, that 's the bitterest sting!
For your sake.

ILDICO
For my sake, yes, for my sake.

SIGISMUND
Have you no shame to feel and to be stung?
— Ah! do you dream of empire, and with him.
Because you own a corner of his mind
And are the last thing that has pleased his eye.
To-morrow loathed, enjoyed, and cast away?

ILDICO
No more of outrage.

SIGISMUND
Ildico, I love you
To my life's end. I am mad with love and hate!

ILDICO
Sigismund, he will crush you with his heel.
Go.

SIGISMUND
Never will I see you bride of him!
Either he dies, or I.

ILDICO
Go!

[**SIGISMUND** goes out. **ATTILA** returns.

ATTILA
Ildico!
If these few mutinous swords had been a thousand,
This petty tumult the whole world in arms,
I would have borne you from the midst Mine, mine!
Tis written in the unalterable stars.
I have heard to-night God crying out of heaven

'Ildico, Ildico!'

ILDICO
Not yet, not yet!

ATTILA
Now! For Heaven puts from me the wife I had.
A curse is on her, but on you the choice.
The oracle has spoken; we are bound
In destiny together. O, by my soul
I love you!

ILDICO
Is it written so, past strength
To break or alter, past all strength of will.
Of fear, of anguish?

ATTILA
It is written so;
You shall be mine.

ILDICO
My captain and my King!
Let me not think: I totter. O blind me, blind me
In love that burns up all I cast away!
Let it all burn, and one great single flame
Clothe us for ever! Hide me, thou strong tower!

[She buries her head in his breast, then looks up.

ATTILA
My love is fierce, never will let thee go.

ILDICO
O turn not eyes so terrible on me!

ATTILA
Ah! seest thou, seest thou? — Give me back my sons!
Thou bitter sweet, canst thou so much atone?
Canst thou? Thou shalt! Heaven swears it me, thou shalt!
Down, images of terror, to the gulf
You sprang from! I defy you! Here and here
Out of black night I kiss thee, life for life.

ILDICO
What agony shakes from you such wild words?
What haggard sights are staring?

ATTILA
Scorching leaves,
Where hundred hopes were green! Thou hast
slain my sons.

ILDICO
I?

ATTILA
Thou.

ILDICO
They live.

ATTILA
The flutter of a spark,
No more. The hour 's dated. They are sentenced.
When thou didst come, shining across my path,
God hung their doom in heaven, a fiery sign

ILDICO
Look where the black-winged clouds have fleeted off—
Yonder it burns again!

ATTILA
By that bright doom,
By my soul's waste and desert, by the pang,
The loss, the fury, thou shalt all avenge.
Thou famine and thou feast, thou desolation
And thou all future joy!

[Putting a torch above her head.

Stand in the light.
Thou challenge of mortality, thou Queen!
Is it of mortal stuff that thou art made,
That housest Time's great secret?

Wound and bliss.
Cruel and precious with the cost of death,
I kiss thy robe.
Thou nourisher and mould of kings to be.

ILDICO
Ah! take my body, take my soul, take all
I am and was and shall be — but a woman.
Only a woman!

ATTILA
Woman, and my bride!
Yon streaming star of loss and death shall change
His omened fire to be our nuptial torch.
The morrow comes

ILDICO
Look how the east is pale!

ATTILA
Dawn! The new day, new heaven, and new earth.
Now Attila has shaken off his sleep
And you shall see him kindled. He whose hand
Holds over us that wonder in the sky
Wields also me. I am the sword. And lo,
Yonder the world that waits us; all the world!

ILDICO
Ah! thither, thither let us speed, my King,
Speed on fast horses: let us drink the wind.
There is no rough fare that shall not be sweet.
No bed not soft, no hardship not delight,
So I am with you. Take me, carry me
Out of all this, out of all this, for ever!

[A trumpet sounds in the distance.

A trumpet in the night!

ATTILA
I know that peal:
It challenges my fate.

ILDICO [Trumpet again; nearer.]
Hark, hark again!

ATTILA
I have heard that sound upon the blood-red field
A hundred times. Ildico, Ildico,
Our horses' hoofs shall stamp the Sacred Street,
And you shall sit throned in the Capitol;
For pleasaunce walks you shall have continents,
For jewels, subject cities

[Trumpet again.]

ILDICO
Attila!

What summons blows? The dawn is breaking.
Hark!

ATTILA
It is Rome's trumpet — You shall reign in Rome.

CURTAIN

ACT III

SCENE I

The same scene as in Act I. Midday. Groups of **PEOPLE** passing by or loitering; among them
BURBA, **ESLA**, and other **HUNS**. Enter from the right **RORIK**, in haste.

BURBA
Rorik!

RORIK
War! By the Dragon, war; we shall have war!
I tell you Attila is stirred at last;
These mouldering days are done.

BURBA
Tell us of the envoys.

ESLA
These Romans

BURBA
Has he sent them packing home
With a challenge? Did he threat them? Did you hear?

RORIK
They have not seen him.

ESLA
How?

RORIK
Refused, contemned!
You shall see them in a minute come this way
With flouted faces muttering anxiously
In one another's ear.

ESLA

He would not see them?
Good!

BURBA
No, 'tis ill.

RORIK
Whichever way, 'tis war.

BURBA
I like it not. His thought 's all Ildico.
To-night he weds her: he 'll have none of war
Nor state affairs; the woman fills his eyes.
He sees nought else. The world may howl for him.

RORIK
A week, and he 'll be sated. Could a woman
Kindle him as last night we saw him kindled?
Did you not note the lightnings in his eye,
And how his words leapt after, quick as thunder?
That was a good night's work — if but he had let me
Slit the long throat of that fool Sigismund!

ESLA
The fellow lurks about still.

BURBA
Yet I doubt.

RORIK
What say you then to this? The Gothic kings
Are summoned hither.

BURBA
To the marriage-feast?

RORIK
They come with armies. Look across the plain.
Yonder 's a moving glitter. It is they!
The spears of Ardaric and Valamir.
Down to the gate!

ESLA
Down to the gate!

RORIK
Witi Come on!

[The **HUNS** go out left.

[A **CROWD** of people come noisily on the scene; followed by the Roman envoys **MESSALLA** and **LAETUS**, before whom the Moorish dwarf **ZERCON** marches with antic gestures.

ZERCON
The King shall hear you. I have power with him.
I have my own cause too that I shall plead.
Trust me, you men of Rome! I wield a sword
And wag a tongue as well.

A MAN
Your champion, Romans!

A WOMAN
Faint hearts, a champion!

MEN and WOMEN
Zercon!

ZERCON
Follow me,
People! I go to give the Gothic kings
My welcome.

[Exeunt all but the **ROMANS**.

LAETUS
Are all mad, or is it we?

MESSALLA
This is the future, Laetus. We are past;
These are our conquerors.

LAETUS
Rome, what a rabble!
Here's all the quartered world jostling in fragments.

MESSALLA
Our mould is cracked; here is the molten ore
Streaming and seething.

LAETUS
Were I Caesar now,
I 'd catch and cage these motley chatterers
And watch their apish antics, for the jest.
And yet our errand 's as fantastical.
I thought it always mad, but madder now.

A princess of the purple, Caesar's sister,
Proffers her troth, her uninvited troth.
To this barbarian; sends a ring to him.
And wooes him, wooes this wild boar in his den.
'Tis a wild story! — Come, we are refused.
Scorned, slighted: what can profit to stay on?
We have seen

MESSALLA
But have not conquered. No, I stay
And win this audience. Attila shall hear.
Will you go back and tell Honoria
'We went, and we did nothing, and return'?

LAETUS
Her pride will rage at this indignity.

MESSALLA
Yes, if we fail, but not if we succeed.
I find that Onegesius the Greek
Contrives all here. I spoke with him apart.
I think — but see, he comes.

[Enter **ONEGESIUS**.

LAETUS
It is all madness.
Well?

MESSALLA
Onegesius
Attila will hear you — upon condition.

MESSALLA
The terms?

ONEGESIUS
A public audience.

MESSALLA
Impossible.

ONEGESIUS
Speak what you will) but speak it before all.
King Attila will hear and welcome you.

MESSALLA
Our matter is for him and him alone.

ONEGESIUS
His ways are open; he keeps no private ear.

LAETUS
Renegade Greek! Let us back to Rome, Messalla.

ONEGESIUS
As you will.

[Exit right.

MESSALLA
Patience!

LAETUS
I am sick of patience!
Do you imagine, were Honoria here
And saw her foolish daydream by daylight,
And found herself a gibe and castaway
Among these hideous Huns, she would endure
An instant? O, post back to Italy!
Think of your garden on the Aventine,
Your library, your fishponds, waiting you

MESSALLA
They are waiting always, Laetus.

[**SIGISMUND**, hurriedly comes up to them.

Who is this?

LAETUS
He stares at us intently.

MESSALLA
Are you a Hun?

SIGISMUND
A Hun! I would rather go upon four legs
Than be a beast on two.

MESSALLA
Yet you are here.

SIGISMUND
This is my land, not theirs.

MESSALLA
Then Attila
You love not?

SIGISMUND
Were my fingers at his throat! —
You are from Rome. He is your enemy
Eternal. You will see him face to face —
O were I you!

MESSALLA
What then?

SIGISMUND [With a gesture]
A little thing.

LAETUS
This is a little thing.

[Showing a dagger.

MESSALLA
Your thoughts run fast.
But Attila refuses us, my friend.
We are dismissed his presence.

SIGISMUND
Attila
Is ruled.

MESSALLA
How?

SIGISMUND
By a woman.

MESSALLA
Who is she?

SIGISMUND
Burgundy's last of royalty, Ildico,
My foster-sister.

LAETUS
What, another princess!
O happy Hun!

SIGISMUND

To-night he weds her.

LAETUS
Weds!

SIGISMUND
Unless — You are Romans, you bring news from Rome,
Business of moment, doubtless, that shall turn
His mind to heavier issues. What is a woman
When policy is in the balance? Go,
Get his ear, divert him. Women love to taste
Their power upon a man. Seek Ildico,
She will persuade him.

LAETUS
Excellent foster-brother!

MESSALLA
Where is this princess?

SIGISMUND
I will bring her to you.

[**SIGISMUND** goes into ildico's house.

LAETUS
Wedded to-night! Honoria's dream 's a dream!
Home again, home: all 's ended, come!

MESSALLA
Not yet.

LAETUS
What?

MESSALLA
Let it be a dream. I never feared
Its coming true, or would have stayed at home.
Attila will deride it, I know well.
But I have promised to Honoria
To give the ring, and I will give the ring.
Moreover, I will see this Hun, whom Rome
Pays tribute of her fear to.

[**ILDICO** comes out attended by **CUNEGONDE** and maids.

LAETUS
O, she 's fair!

ILDICO
Are you from Rome?

MESSALLA
Princess, we are from Rome.

ILDICO
What brings you hither? Do you await the
King?

MESSALLA
We crave a private audience of the King
Which he refuses. Must we go empty away
And say in Rome that Attila

[He hesitates.

ILDICO
Say on.

MESSALLA
That Attila unroyally withholds
His ear from honourable embassies,
Abstaining from that ancient courtesy,
The privilege of kings? Shall we report
That Attila is afraid? Princess, you know
'Tis not so, but I think he is abused
In counsel. Could we see him face to face,
Then would he listen, then would be himself;
But it seems Onegesius holds the power.

ILDICO
Onegesius. I will ask the King. I think
That you shall have your audience. Stay meanwhile.
Fetch some wine hither! Do you refresh yourselves.

[She signs to her **MAIDS** who re-enter the house.

MESSALLA
Princess, we thank you, from our hearts we thank you.

[Exit **ILDICO** into the house of Attila. **CUNEGONDE** remains in the background.

LAETUS
Who would have sought such beauty here? — She rules him.

MESSALLA

For the moment.

LAETUS
What new thought possesses you?

MESSALLA
I listen: I can hear the coming roar
Of chaos, when the keystone 's struck away
From this rude arch of empire.

LAETUS
Attila?
Give that Burgundian opportunity —

[Two **MAIDS** return, bringing wine and cakes on gold dishes, then retire.

I am weary. Drink! To the fair Ildico!

[He drinks but sets dawn the cup with a wry face.

And may she come not to as sour an end!
O, golden dishes!

[Nibbles at a cake.

MESSALLA
What was in that sigh?

LAETUS
Nothing; a memory. A bath, Messalla,
Some olives, and a bath!

ILDICO [Re-entering]
King Attila
Gives audience — but to one.

LAETUS
Not both?

ILDICO
To one.

LAETUS
Then you, Messalla.

MESSALLA
Now?

ILDICO
Immediately.

MESSALLA
Thanks, noble princess, for your intercession.
Would that our gratitude could match your grace!

[Exit **MESSALLA**.

ILDICO
Tell me of Rome.

LAETUS
What shall I say? A city
That is utterly aweary of itself.
Why, did you pace upon the Roman streets,
You 'd find yourself a wonder; next, a worship;
Flowers, odes, a hundred lovers at your feet;
And on the morrow, nothing: out-of-date,
A yesterday; we love not yesterdays.
We live for pleasure, princess — a hard life!

ILDICO
Is every Roman so? Yet Rome is feared.
Is there no pith and mettle in her sons?
No spirit and no daring?

LAETUS
I have heard
Those words, but never used them, mettle and daring;
And it was on such lovely lips as yours
I heard them last, with such indignant tone. —
Rome boasts a princess whom our poets hymn
The moon of Italy, the rose of fame.
Though I would swear the face I look upon
Would turn them traitors.

ILDICO
Only a woman, then?
Does it not shame you to be called a man?
How is she named?

LAETUS
Honoria.

ILDICO
And a princess?

LAETUS
The Emperor's sister.

ILDICO
She should be your queen —
O, can you not catch fire from such a heart?

LAETUS
'Tis prettier pleasure to see others burn
Than burn oneself. Unhappy Honoria!

ILDICO
Unhappy? I perceive this is a soul
You cannot understand, of purest flame
That wastes itself unfuelled; yet I think
She is happier than you that mock at her.

LAETUS
She is unhappy, for she sits and sighs
Beside her palace window all day long.
And gazing over roofs and roar of Rome
Dreams of a hero, fancying, poor she.
If the north wind blow, it may bring her news
Of Attila.

ILDICO
Of Attila!

LAETUS
Her hero.
Her Attila, her world-subduing king,
Whose name is text and comment on our ways,
Whose greatness canopies the day, the night.
And puts the stars out Ah, mere dreams, mere dreams!
Unhappy she! Your fame shall make Rome envious!
Princess,
More happy than Honoria, farewell!

[Exit **LAETUS**. **CUNEGONDE** comes forward.

ILDICO [Coldly]
Ah, **CUNEGONDE**!

CUNEGONDE
I heard.

ILDICO
If this be a Roman,

Rome is a bubble.

CUNEGONDE
And Honoria?
This lady that has all men at her feet—

ILDICO
What of her?

CUNEGONDE
Nothing.

ILDICO
Tell me, what of her?

CUNEGONDE
This only, that she loves your Attila,
And sends these envoys

ILDICO
She! High state affairs,
Not woman's messages they come upon.

CUNEGONDE
And yet

ILDICO
No more. Go!

[Exit **CUNEGONDE**.

Now, if that were true.
And Attila listen? Shame, O shame for me! —
O what is love, that we should speak of it
So fair and fondly? It is fierce, not kind;
Cruel, not tender; 'tis not a thing we own;
It clutches us, and will not let us go;
It is a stream we drown in, a strong stream
That sweeps us out of sight of home, of friends.
Of our own souls, of everything.
[With sudden change of tone]
'Tis written
In heaven that I am his, my Attila's;
A bond unbreakable, and in that bond
My body is made holy to him, and I
More wonderful than woman.
Honoria?
The truth! I 'll seek him; I must know the truth!

[Exit right.

An audience-chamber, plainly furnished, **ATTILA** is seated on a law dais, left, **MESSALLA** stands at the right, the **SLAVE** who carries the treasure stands behind. At the back a curtained door. **MESSALLA** has just finished speaking.

ATTILA
I find no matter for my private ear
In this. I think my patience is abused.

MESSALLA
My prologue 's ended. But for what 's to come
I crave your secrecy: this is a theme
Nearer and more familiar. But meanwhile
Let Attila accept a gift from Rome. —
Pour out your treasure, slave, at the King's feet.

[The **SLAVE** advances but is stopped by a gesture from **ATTILA**.

ATTILA
Hold! Come no nearer. Leave the treasure there.
Dismiss the slave. We are alone. Speak on.
How, hesitating? Do you moisten lips
For this that was so instant to be said?

MESSALLA
I doubt to find the words that shall commend
My mission.

ATTILA
State affairs are suited best,
With plain words. What would the Emperor with me?

MESSALLA
Your pardon! I must seek to tune my speech
To other issues, though an old man's lips
Discourse them strangely; yet, if I am old,
I have seen the more, and ageing with my kind
Know nothing 's strange that 's human. Wisdom is
Not to despise: the thread of fate, wherein
Events are bound and huge dominions hang.
Is often spun of tissue delicate
As sighs, as dreams, a thread that one might burst

Against the beating of a woman's heart.

ATTILA
Come, come! What would you speak of?

MESSALLA
Of a woman.
It is a woman uses speech in me.

ATTILA
Is Rome so manless and emasculate
That women send ambassadors?

MESSALLA
Hear yet
Before you judge, O Attila. It is
A woman, but imperial, sends me hither.
You know the Emperor has a sister, young,
A ripe eighteen — Honoria; she is one
Whose nature will not starve in custom's mould,
But breaks in precious fire — how shall I say?
You will not understand how I am moved
In speaking of her; a spirit that rebels
From seeming what she is not, chooses, wills.
And stops not at the halting-place of fear.
Whatever moves her, moves her to the quick.
She is proud; yet giving, she gives absolutely:
Her nature is a queen. And Caesar fears her,
Grudges her scope, sets spies upon her, mews
Her wings in palace walls that prison her;
Even now debates within some convent's gate
For ever to exile her.

ATTILA
What of this?
Caesar may dungeon half a hundred sisters,
I will not stir to help or draw the bolt.
What 's this to me?

MESSALLA
Alas! upon this theme
My tongue grows garrulous. Then, to be brief.
This young, imperious, and unmated heart.
Finding about her none to incarnate
The greatness that she dreams of, — for she dreams
Of such a Caesar as the Julian star
Mourned, when the master of all nations fell —
Would sponge away five hundred years, to breathe

Heroic times again, and living caged
Fosters the more such fancies as, you know.
Flower in a prison, wither in the world, —
She turns from Rome to far horizons: there
She hears one name fill all the North with dread,
The rumour of one spirit matching hers
In greatness of adventure and desire.

ATTILA
Whom do you speak of?

MESSALLA
Whom but Attila?
As queen to king, she sends her embassage;
Proudly and freely thus declares her heart.
Honoria weds with Attila or none;
In proof and pledge whereof she sends this ring
Affiancing her heart and destiny.

ATTILA
Give me the ring. What story or device
Is wrought upon the gem?

MESSALLA
It shows the fleece
Old poets tell of, like that bearded star
We watched last night, hung golden in the gloom
Of jealous forests, and the dragon coiled
About the tree-trunk with a burning eye.
Apollodorus, the Sicilian, made
The gem: for modern workmanship 'tis well,
Though I could show you in my cabinet

ATTILA [With sudden change of tone]
What talk is this of toys and girls and rings?
Say now what business brought you?

MESSALLA
All is said.
A girl's whim, doubtless, 'tis but a girl's whim.
She should have paced an ampler age than ours.
We maim her, a proud marble of old time
In dust and wreck found beautiful, but maimed;
But I — I am her friend, and for my friendship
She chose me for this errand, and because
My years perhaps seemed fitter to commend
Her act as not a folly, though a folly
To Attila it is; and if 'tis so

She is answered: but to Attila's own ear
I have committed it; my duty 's done.

ATTILA [Starting up]
So with this patched and most unlikely tale
You thought to blind me, and behind this mask
Of trumpery and words to carry off
Your baffled plot! You have not fooled me. No,
Your errand was my murder!

MESSALLA
God forbid!

ATTILA
Am I a dolt! A round-eyed innocent!
That know not your Italian practices?
'Twas tried before: Byzantium bribed a man
To stab me in close audience; now 'tis Rome.
You meant to do it while that slave of yours
Poured out the gold and while I fingered it.

MESSALLA
I swear

ATTILA
What were you hired with to remove
Rome's nightmare, and pull down the hated Hun?
Why, Caesar's purple, Valentinian's throne
Were less than just reward!

MESSALLA
King, I confess,
Were Attila no more, Rome would sleep sounder;
But not a Roman stirred a finger here.

ATTILA
I say, my death was plotted ere you came.
Ay, chuckled over in the Capitol!

MESSALLA
Not so, I swear, no, nor a dream of it.
I come, ambassador to Attila,
And with no thought but of my embassy.
An office sacred out of time to kings,
As mine should be to you.

ATTILA
Ambassador!

Embassy from a girl — a shameless girl,
If what you say be truth; if truth, 'tis folly
That merits no respect; but it is false.
Pretence and pretext. Do you think to escape
Because you are foiled, or that I honour names
Put on for cloaks, or spare because you are old —
The older, the worse fool?

[Calling **RORIK**, who appears instantly.

Take out this man,
And tie him up to be an archer's mark, —
My Huns have lacked a target — and proclaim.
Thus Attila deals with traitors, and with spies
Usurping honourable offices.

MESSALLA
So be it: let my death dishonour you,
Attila. No matter: my term 's ripe.
A Roman dies — but Rome remains.

ATTILA
Come back.
I have a word yet. — Rorik, wait without.

[After a pause.

I did not think Rome bred such spirits still;
Come, sir, be open. Coward you are not,
Nor should be fool. Put off the mask: you are free.
What deeper purpose brings you to this place?
No hand shall harm you, so you tell me all.

MESSALLA
It is all told, condemn it as you will
For folly or for fiction; truth it is
Princess Honoria sent you the ring.
Praying me earnestly to deliver it
Into your very hands; nothing but this
Was my commission, nothing else my purpose.

ATTILA [To himself]
It 's true, then, this mad story of the ring.
A woman, again a woman!
[To **MESSALLA**] What's your name?

MESSALLA
Messalla.

ATTILA
Go, Messalla; you have seen
That Attila is armed, yet can be mild.
Go back to Rome

MESSALLA
If I am free to go,
I pray you, let me take the ring again,
Honoria's silent and sufficient answer.

ATTILA
No; tell your princess I accept the ring,
'Tis on my finger, say you saw it there,
And say besides that at my chosen time
I come to claim her. How, not pleased? What 's ill?
Pluck laurel for your brows, ambassador!
Honoria shall crown you.

[Calling to **RORIK**, who appears.

Rorik, give
This Roman escort. He is free.

[Exit **MESSALLA** with **RORIK**.

Bald fool!
If this be she Fate points her finger at.
Not Ildico, but she? A Roman girl,
Essenced and puny, and that has no shame
To cast herself before an unknown man!
Such women please me not at all. And yet
Rome on my finger! The gem glitters at me.
A world of cities, old and populous.
The ports of traffic with wide seas between,
Enfortressed armies, tributary kings.
Rivers and corn-lands, mountains veined with gold,
The hopes, the fears of hundred nations, all
Contracted to one point of changing light
Upon my finger.
[Calling]
Onegesius!
What was it the sorcerer said? A woman, a woman!
Enemy born, yet may be turned to boon.
Honoria chimes as well as Ildico.
Doubt wins upon my soul, but it is she.

[A **SLAVE** enters.

Call Onegesius!— Must I dance a puppet
And women pull the strings? I? What's one woman
More than another?

[**ILDICO** enters.

O, she comes!

ILDICO
My lord,
Am I admitted now? What is afoot?
Tell me — your brows are knitted — tell your bride
What brought these Romans hither?

ATTILA
State affairs.

ILDICO
Trouble?

ATTILA
No trouble.

ILDICO
Good, then?

ATTILA
Who can tell?
But there 's no trouble possible, when my eyes
Have joy of you, my Ildico.

ILDICO
My lord,
Is it true you love me?

[**ONEGESIUS** enters.

ATTILA
Doubt all else but that.

ILDICO
Even to the end?

ATTILA
Even to the end. But see,
Grave counsels call me. Onegesius comes.
We must unravel intricate affairs —

And then to feast; and then

ILDICO
Have you no more
To tell me?

ATTILA
Till to-night, sweet, till to-night!

[**ILDICO** goes out slowly. **ONEGESIUS** comes forward.

Is she not fair?

ONEGESIUS
Too fair not to be feared.
But you 'll not hear me.

ATTILA
Is she not a shape
To body forth the purposes of Gods?
Can they create such meaning to the eye,
Inscribe all-glorious hopes and histories
On form and feature, but to gull the soul
That is the eye's dupe? O, I doubt she 's nothing!
Mortal flesh, a fair body, nothing more! —
Fetch me that sorcerer, I have need of him.

ONEGESIUS
He is dead.

ATTILA
Since when?

ONEGESIUS
He died at your command.

ATTILA
I never ordered—

ONEGESIUS
But consented.

ATTILA
O,
By plague and thunder, you have served me ill!

ONEGESIUS
What need to ply him further? All is known.

The oracle 's already part fulfilled,
The rest 's to come.

ATTILA
I tell you, all 's not known.
Look on my hand.

ONEGESIUS
A ring!

ATTILA
A Roman ring,
A gift.

ONEGESIUS
From Caesar?

ATTILA
No, from Caesar's sister.

ONEGESIUS
Honoria?

ATTILA
She. And with the ring she gives
Her heart and fate, her body and her soul.
What say you?

ONEGESIUS
Rome itself is in the ring.
The imperial hostage! 'Tis an army
Given over to you in the enemy's camp. —
Why, this speaks clearer than all oracles
Rome shall be yours.

ATTILA
Think you so? Think you so?
'Tis like the silent action of immortals
To crown us with the long despaired of prize.
I have heard of stars that tumbled in the lap
Of despised women, and enthroned them queens.
But O, to pluck and wrench this rooted joy
Out of my breast! Honoria 's a name
Unwelcomed, thrust on me: but Ildico —
Her lips have been on mine, and I had built
An image high as heaven in desire
Of her fulfilling soul. — Well, crumble, dreams!
Be it only her sweet body, she is mine!

Are the armies summoned?

ONEGESIUS
Valamir and Ardaric
Are come, their hosts are camped at hand.

ATTILA
Tis well.
Hernak yet lives. What if the omens lied?
My curse on weakness that entreats for signs
And promises contemptuously cast
As bones to dogs! These double-dealing Fates
Laugh at us, when we dread them. From this hour
They shall dread me. Let shifting omens point
To Ildico or to Honoria,
I laugh, for both are given me, both are mine!

ONEGESIUS
Nay, take my counsel: choose. To clutch at both
May be to lose both.

ATTILA
By this glittering ring
I will have Rome. — Take means to set on foot.
To-morrow, our preparation for the march.
And Ildico—

ONEGESIUS
Forswear her, Attila.

ATTILA
Tumble the towers of earth and heaven, not I!
No, though the superstitious glory 's gone,
She 's my possession. If the world is mine
To break within my hands, shall I renounce
The spice and sting that 's at the core of it?

ONEGESIUS
Ay, better so, when the Gods give you Rome.

ATTILA
Onegesius, hark! We that rode over earth
And trod it down, we are masters; shall not we
Invade these Powers that lurk within the cave
Of time to be, and mock and baffle us?
Show me the thing that boldness cannot quell!
I swear, did we burst in, our swords should find
Fate cowering there.

ONEGESIUS
As perilous a world.
Perhaps, you are invading now.

ATTILA
What mean you?

ONEGESIUS
A woman's soul.

ATTILA
O women, women, women!
Flowers to be plucked, — what force is in a flower
To harm or to be feared? Flowers to be plucked!

CURTAIN

ACT IV

SCENE I

A hall set out with small tables and with a double throne, left, on a dais. At the back, between two pillars, an inner chamber masked by heavy curtains.

As the curtain rises **HERNAK** is discovered seated on the throne alone, **KERKA** enters, right.

KERKA
I have sought you—

HERNAK
I am here.

KERKA
On the king's throne!

HERNAK
One day I must be king.

KERKA [Embracing him]
My noble boy!
In you I live, in you I am avenged.
May she be barren, may she have no child,
She that usurps me! May her beauty be
A flower that withers and is tossed away!
May she too drink the cup that I drink of.

And may it be thrice bitter to her soul!
Son, my own son, live, for I live in you!

HERNAK
Let me go, mother!

KERKA
Hernak, promise me!

HERNAK
What?

KERKA
This: be absent from the feast to-night.

HERNAK
I am to stand upon the King's right hand.

KERKA
Yes; always. But to-night your place shall want you.
The King shall want you and shall ask for you;
But you 'll be absent. For my sake do this.

HERNAK
I was to stand upon the King's right hand.
My father will be angered.
[Relenting]
Yet, I will.
But let me go now; I must seek abroad
Among the captains, for they talk of war.

KERKA
O no, stay by me!
Hark! the music comes.
We must be gone now. Music for her feet!
Nay, swifter, swifter I dance her to her doom!

[A file of **GIRLS** holding above their heads a long white scarf enters in a rhythmical dance preceding **ILDICO**, who takes her stand upon the dais, **KERKA** standing with **HERNAK**, aver against **ILDICO**, right.

Ay, glory now! Be flushed, be blind with bliss!
Heap up the dizzy moment with delight
Ere it be spilt, as soon it shall be spilt.
And thou, supplanter, be supplanted! Then
Shalt thou come hither where now Kerka stands,
With no son by thy side; that haughty head
Be humble, and thou discarded and abhorred;
And then the Roman woman in thy place

ILDICO [Speaking in exaltation]
I fear not any woman upon earth.
I have that certainty within my soul
Which mocks at past and future. So, hate on.
I pity thee, so poisoned.

KERKA
Pity rather
Thine own awakening to reality.
With thy lost faith fixed on a faithless man.

ILDICO
Fixed in the great heavens shines unchangeable
My destiny for ever.

[Music. The **HUNS** begin to troop in to the banquet, chanting the conclusion of a war song.

Where the Dragon-banner streamed,
Armies quaked and rolled asunder;
Lightnings on our lances gleamed,
Cities splintered at our thunder.

Riding like the whirlwind's breath
We were Famine, we were Death;
Send us such another day»
Attila, our Attila!

[As the **HUNS** take their seats **ARDARIC** and **VALAMIR** come in and occupy each a high seat. **ATTILA** enters, holding out his arms to **HERNAK**, who turns from him and goes out with **KERKA**. **ATTILA** with a laugh passes on to the throne.]

ATTILA
Kings, princes, warriors, whose assembling swords
Array our bridal banquet, welcome all!
Out of our birth-land of remotest East
What goad of God has pricked us, and driven on,
A storm against all storms, like thunder-wind,
Hither across uncounted plains and streams
You know; and here a white flower of the West
To my rough soul, so lately scarred with loss.
Brings balsam, and my fortune crowns afresh.
Heaven prophesied this in yon sudden star.
Behold my bride, the gentle Ildico!
Behold your queen, the noble Ildico!
Pledge us in wine, in the red wine, my Huns,
To your queen; drink! To the fair Ildico!

HUNS
Attila, hail! Ildico, hail! Attila and Ildico, hail! hail!

ESLA
No word of war.

RORIK
Wait, there 's a word to come.

BURBA
Ill comes of wedding with a Western bride.

ILDICO [Rising]
My King, I pledge thee in the cup, and drink
To the glory of Attila.

HUNS
Attila, Attila!

ILDICO
Where your King rides, there Ildico will ride.

ESLA
Hear you that, Burba? Royal as she 's fair!

ATTILA
Wine, kings and captains, let the wine go round.
Laugh your full hearts out, revel at your ease.
No trumpet cries us to the field to-night.
No, nor to-morrow. Come, a long regale.
That tosses care into the dancing cup.
The cup of mirth and joy.

[Movement of disappointment among the **HUNS**.

BURBA
Pah, fondling hands!
He dotes upon her with a glistening eye.

[**ZERCON** enters, martially arrayed in grotesque magnificence amid the laughter of the **BANQUETERS**.

ZERCON
Majesty, a boon!

[He draws his sword with a fierce air as a **HUN** intercepts him.

Fellow, my falchion 's bare!
Hands off, or I shall split you, crown to fork!

RORIK
Toss the imp to me.

ZERCON
Majesty, a boon!

ATTILA
A song, then, for the boon.

HUNS
Zercon, a song!

ZERCON
I mouth no songs; I am a man of deeds.

HUNS
Zercon, a song! A battle-song, a war-song!

ATTILA
Let the knave speak.

ZERCON
O King, this night gives you
A wife, but me it robs; I had a wife.
A yellow Goth has stolen her from me.
Avenge me!

RORIK
Man of deeds!

ZERCON
The monster fled;
He feared me.

ATTILA
You shall have another wife.
And I will choose her. Women are the spoils
For heroes, Zercon.

ZERCON
The King's choice for me!
Most bounteous thanks. Some wine, give me some wine!

HUNS
A song, a war-song!

RORIK

War!

ATTILA
What, still untuned
To revel! Does the bull stamp in the stall?
Drink deeper! Camps of mire in the foul fog
And sinew-biting frost, — would you have all
You toiled in, rather than the toil's reward?
Feast and carouse! Bethink you of the drouth.
The fiery dust, the thirsts unquenchable.
Then relish the full beaker! Parch your throats
With hot remembrance, that the flooding wine
May drown it. Come, unharness those swift thoughts.
Tastes not the wine well? Must you hear the sound
Of axe and arrow ere you savour it?

RORIK
Now mark!

ATTILA
Forget! can you not quite forget
Music of battle, sword on helmet ringing,
Spear dinting shield?

A HUN
Give us that sound again

BURBA
Then we will revel!

RORIK
Swords for Attila!

HUNS
'Send us such another day,
Attila, our Attila!'

[The **HUNS** raise their swords, and gather nearer **ATTILA**.

ATTILA
Huns!

ESLA
The King speaks.

ATTILA
Huns!

MANY VOICES
Hark to Attila!

ATTILA
Huns, that have over-ridden earth with me,
Will you not rest?

HUNS
Never!

ATTILA
Nor sit at ease,
Warriors of mine? The pleasant earth is yours.

HUNS
To horse, to battle! Let us ride again!

ATTILA
Huns, I exult to see you, hear you, feel you.
When I have reined my horse in, stamping earth
Before the charge, and quivering in the flank,
So have I felt a mettle answer mine.
As now in you it answers.

RORIK
War at last!

ATTILA
What! Did you deem me idle, sleep-benumbed
And sloth -corrupted? Me? Then know my soul
Smouldered, because it burned more deep within;
And while you chafed and muttered — did you not? —
My purpose swelled and ripened. The hour strikes
To show it

HUNS
Show it us!

ATTILA
King Ardaric,
How many spears are counted in your host?

ARDARIC
Five thousand by the river, and seven times more
Beyond the pass.

ATTILA
King Valamir, say you

How many can you add?

VALAMIR
Not a man less
Than thirty thousand for my summons wait
Beside the ford of Danube.

ATTILA
Huns, you hear?
Now, Hun and Goth and Gepid, since the time
Chimes with your temper, and my mood with both,
Behold the Sword!

[He shows the sacred sword at his belt, and drawing it, holds it erect.

ALL
The Sword of God!

ATTILA
You know
My meaning. When this Sword is girded on.
You know my vows are taken, and my resolve
Not put from me till this is put from me:
And my will holds to march.

ALL
Whither, whither?

ATTILA
Attila
On Rome!

ALL
On Rome! Rome shall be ours!
Rome! Rome!

[Amid the excited cries of the **HUNS**, **SIGISMUND** suddenly enters.

SIGISMUND
Huns, let a word be spoken in your midst
Of one that tasted your King's clemency.
To-night he weds with a Burgundian bride:
Shall Burgundy be silent? Here and now
I dedicate my sword to Attila.

[Drawing his sword he rushes at **ATTILA**. **ILDICO** throws herself in his way but **SIGISMUND** is at once cut down by the **HUNS**.

ILDICO
Sigismund!

SIGISMUND [Expiring]
Ildico! traitress Ildico!

[A black cloak is flung over the body which is carried out while **ATTILA** speaks.

ATTILA
A victim, Huns! A victim that the Gods
Slay for my glory. He who seeks my life
Finds his own doom. Not twice nor thrice a stab
Has meant me and has failed. An omen, Huns, —
The Gods, the Gods have Attila in charge, —
An omen on the threshold of our war.
Let not this fool's irruption on our feast
Distaste your mirth and cloud your revelry;
Yet, for my bride's sake, to your several homes
Pass and disperse. To-night is for the feast.
To-morrow trumpets us to Italy,
And greets us in the saddle with the sun.

[The **HUNS** pass out clashing shields and crying 'Rome! Rome!' **ILDICO** has been standing transfixed with horror, **ATTILA** turns to her exulting.

Now, crown of joys!

ILDICO
Thy spilt blood curses me.
O that 'twas I had fallen at your feet.
Pierced by his steel, my body given for you!

ATTILA
What, yon poor madman, gulping at his doom?
For simple serpents and contriving doves
There is no room in nature but for us.

ILDICO
Attila, I gave, and you have taken.
I have cast away all, all that was my own, —
See, my own blood judges and curses me! —
Say it again, say it is willed in Heaven,
Say that you love me! By that starry bond.
That bond of faith which knots us even to death.
Give me oblivion, give me

ATTILA [Suddenly seizing her in his arms]
Ildico!

ILDICO
Hold me and hide me and drown me in your love.
The greatness and the glory of your love!

ATTILA
Toss all away that burns not in this kiss —
Be strained, you sweetness, strained into my arms.
They shall crush out remembrance into wine
Of ecstasy so fierce you shall not think.
Fear, hope, remember, in the pangs of joy!
I 'd cast a kingdom in the seas to-night.
For the Gods envy me.

[Holding her at arm's length.

O never yet
In teeming Time was such a beauty born
As lives in you and flames. It stings, it maddens!
Thou red wine, I will drink thee!

ILDICO [Catching his hand to hold him off]
Ah, you hurt!
— What is that ring upon your hand? Not mine!

ATTILA
No, but 'tis mine. Do you covet it, the gem?
See in the core of it a winking fire
Glows like a dragon's eye; now it is changed
To colder than a moonbeam, splintered ice.
And now again all angry.

ILDICO
Give it me!

ATTILA
It ravishes your eye? It is from Rome.
A cunning craftsman made it.

ILDICO
Rome? From Rome?
Honoria, Honoria sent it you!

ATTILA
Who has blabbed? What know you of Honoria?
No matter, it is mine.

ILDICO

Fling it away!

ATTILA
Ha, ha!
A dream-sick girl, mewed in a palace cage.
That hunts her wandering fancy on the wind.
And dotes upon a man she never saw —
A milky-hearted girl, in love with dreams.
She sends me this.
Give me the ring!

ILDICO
You suffer it? Accept?
Give me the ring!

ATTILA
What will you do with it?

ILDICO
Trample it with my heel, grind it to dust.
Since you forget my honour and your own.

ATTILA
Soft, soft; I keep it for my uses, sweet, —
State matters you 've no need acquaintance of.
Let the toy be, I shall not wear it more
Till.

ILDICO
Perjury! If any meaning lives
In such a token, such a gift, this hand
Is false, and plighted to Honoria.
This was the Roman's errand that you hid
So secret, and for this you march on Rome
Nor tell your bride a word! O perjured hand!
— I 'll not believe it! Say you jest Tis cruel
To jest so, yet I 'll pardon.

ATTILA
Ay, a jest,
A good jest!

ILDICO
Then give me the ring.

ATTILA
Not now.
Another time. We waste our life's delight.

This night 's for sweeter use than argument.
Come, kiss and pardon.

ILDICO
No, you love me not!
You love me not, that wear another's ring.
Exile me from your inmost purposes.
And tell me last what you should tell me first —
Me whom you vowed the passion of your fate.
Queen of your destiny, your soul, your star

ATTILA
The stars are broken; I am destiny.
In the night's crooked characters let fools
Read their own folly.

ILDICO
Is it nothing, all
You vowed to me beneath that burning star
With earnest eyes and dedicating lips,
Prophecies that entwined us to all time,
False?

ATTILA
A false prophet gulled me with his lies.
I am I, and you are mine.

ILDICO
You love not me!

ATTILA
O, by all torments of desire, I do!

ILDICO
False!

ATTILA
Yes, all 's false but beauty; all is false,
A wilderness of falsehood, but your hair
That stings me, and the crimson of your mouth.
And white throat, and warm panting of your breast —
And they are mine, they shall be mine, mine!
Hark!
How my Huns revel! We will plumb a well
Of bliss beyond their thought.

ILDICO [Breaking violently from him]
O shame, O shame!

A woman such as you would toss to wive
With that misfeatured Moor. False, false, false!

ATTILA
Ah!
Stand so, and let the lovely anger blaze!
I'll not begrudge it fuel. Let it spark
Cheek and eye; beauty is thrice beautiful
So passionately coloured. I am drunk
With joy of gazing on this beauty. — Yet,
Where I am, I am master; and these arms
Can crush as well as cherish. So, be taught.
Come, come! I did but tease that angry mood.
Here are your maids to tire you. Wait me quickly.

[**ATTILA** goes out as **CUNEGONDE** enters with attendant **WOMEN**.

ILDICO
A moment, yet a moment, Cunegonde!

[**CUNEGONDE** retires.

Traitress! No, no! I am not that, no, no!
All terror is come true. It must be done!

[She kneels down and prays.

Gods of my fathers, I have sinned against you:
My eyes were blinded, and I could not see.
Change this distempered fever, that I thought
Was love, and noble; purge it from my heart;
Let me be clean. O, if you did withhold
Your presence for this time, now doubly fill
My soul, my veins! Lift me from weakness up.
O send me strength, strength, agony, but strength!
Let me not now be humbled by this man;
Let me be one remembrance of my blood
That never yet was vile or bore a shame.
And being shamed rises to be avenged.
Make these hands strong to strike him!

{Rising and calling to **CUNEGONDE**.

Cunegonde!

[**CUNEGONDE**, **GISLA**, and **MAIDS** enter with robes, a silver mirror etc. During this scene **CUNEGONDE**
speaks with intense and bitter irony.

Take off this robe!
It weighs me down.

CUNEGONDE
This robe is the King's gift.
It is woven of one piece; the hands that sewed
Were hands of princesses, as smooth as flowers.
Of Eastern princesses, of captive queens.
It has been charmed and hallowed. The world's empress
Might covet such a gift.

ILDICO [Throwing' it front her]
The robe is soiled!
Take off these jewels.

CUNEGONDE
Jewels of such price
Would ransom twenty captains — who shall say
How far outvalue one man's lifeblood spilt
For his country!

ILDICO
Cunegonde!

[To the **MAIDS**.

Go, one of you,
Fetch me that jewel which my mother wore.

GISLA
Of simple bronze? It is not royal gold

CUNEGONDE
Befitting for the bride of Attila!

ILDICO [To the **MAIDS** one of whom goes to fetch the Jewel]
Do as I ask.
[To **GISLA**]
Is not your father sick?
You should be tending upon him, not me.

GISLA
The mirror. Queen!

ILDICO [Holding the mirror]
Is it I?

GISLA

You are changed to-night.
Your gaze is starry, you are far from us.

[All the **MAIDS** but **CUNEGONDE** retire.

ILDICO
I am ready. — Sooner than a mouth of shame
He shall kiss death.

CUNEGONDE [Kneeling and kissing **ILDICO'S** hand]
I have wronged you, O my Queen!
Pardon!

ILDICO [Moving as if to throw her arms round **CUNEGONDE**, then checking herself, fearful of losing self-control]
Good-night! Go!

[The bolting of a door is heard.

Go!

[**CUNEGONDE** goes out. **ILDICO** stands motionless.

The end of the world!

[With sudden excitement]

I have no weapon!
Now,
You Gods, if there be justice, answer me!

[She turns, hearing the step of **ATTILA** approaching and as he enters unarmoured faces him very calm. She sees the sword still at his belt, and her face is illuminated.

ATTILA [with astonishment and admiration in his voice]
Thou miracle! Thou vision! Ildico!
No word? I like thy coldness, my chaste bride.
I swear thy anger did not shine more fair
Than now — light breathes so through the end of rain —
Comes thy submission. Lead me in, my bride!

ILDICO
My lord, command me. Do you wear a sword?

ATTILA
The sword that fell from heaven. I have bound it on
Because my vows are taken; but to-night
Your fingers shall unbuckle it.

ILDICO [Kneeling and unfastening the sword]
Is it true
That Attila is proof to every blade
But this?

ATTILA [Laughing]
My Huns believe it, Ildico.

ILDICO
It is heavy.

ATTILA
With my fate. — Beyond this night
Who knows what waits me, what the storm of hours
Shall hurry me to meet, when the great thunders
Are breaking, and earth crimsoned, far and far.
To what wild seashores of the world? Come all
To-night my heart sits on an easy throne,
Joy fills me, and love fills me; I am filled
With joy of you, my bride, my Ildico.
I am come into my kingdom. Lead me in!

[They pass in together **ILDICO** bearing the sword, to the inner chamber. The stage is left empty. Noise of the **HUNS** revelling without is faintly heard, changed suddenly to a different tone, as exclamations and questions rise to a dull uproar, coming closer. Out of the confusion at last distinct cries are heard:-

Hernak! The King! Hernak! They have killed Hernak!

Voice of RORIK
Knock on the door!

Voice of a HUN
I dare not!

Voice of RORIK
He shall know!
The King shall know that they have slain his son!
Open!

[**ILDICO** glides out of the inner chamber and crouches panting.

ILDICO
I struck so hard, the hilt has hurt my hand!.
Horrible vision, leap not out at me!
It was not I that did it! I am weak!
And my hands tremble, tremble!

Voice of RORIK
Burst the bolt!

ILDICO
Ah! terrible strong Gods that raised me up.
Fling me not down, cast me not quite away!

[The door is burst open. She rises to her full height. **RORIK** and other **HUNS** with swords and torches rush in.

RORIK
The King!

ESLA
Hernak is slain!

RORIK
Where is the King?

ILDICO
Go back, go back! You shall not enter here.
I have killed him, I have killed him! He is dead!

[**RORIK** passes her and goes to the inner chamber, then staggers back as if struck.

ESLA
What shakes you?

RORIK
Tell me that I dreamed, not saw!

ESLA [Looking in and returning]
The Sword is in his heart, — the Sword of God!

ILDICO
Here, here in me! Bury your blades in me!

ESLA
She is mad with horror.

RORIK
Attila is dead.
And God has slain him, God has smitten him!

[They pass out into the crowd without; wails and furious cries repeat themselves into the far distance.

ILDICO [Listening transfixed]

The pillar of the world is broken down:
And yet heaven has not fallen! O Attila! . . .
Gods of my country, now you are avenged!

CURTAIN

Laurence Binyon – A Short Biography

Robert Laurence Binyon, CH, was born on August 10th, 1869 in Lancaster in Lancashire, England to Quaker parents, Frederick Binyon and Mary Dockray.

He studied at St Paul's School, London before enrolling at Trinity College, Oxford, to read classics.

Binyon's first published work was Persephone in 1890. Whilst only a few pages in length it certainly illustrated the talents that Binyon would develop as a poet even though he continued to advance multiple career opportunities.

Immediately after graduating in 1893, Binyon started work at the British Museum for the Department of Printed Books, writing catalogues for the museum and art monographs for himself. As well as being one of England's best poets he was also renowned for his knowledge of various arts particularly with regard to Japan and Persia.

His first poetry book Lyric Poems was published in 1894.

In 1895 his first art book, Dutch Etchers of the Seventeenth Century, was published and, that same year, Binyon moved into the Museum's Department of Prints and Drawings.

Whilst Binyon became known to a wide audience as a poet his output was not prodigious. In 1898, Porphyrion & Other Poems was published followed by Odes (1901) and The Death of Adam & Other Poems (1904).

That same year, 1904, Binyon married the historian Cicely Margaret Powell. The union was to produce three daughters.

In the early years of the 20th Century Binyon was a regular patron of the Wiener Cafe of London together with fellow artists and intellectuals; Ezra Pound, Sir William Rothenstein, Walter Sickert, Charles Ricketts, Lucien Pissarro and Edmund Dulac.

His poetic work continued despite the demands of the British Museum and his other interests. London Visions was published in 1908 followed by England & Other Poems in 1909.

His work at the British Museum ensured promotions were a frequent occurrence for Binyon. In 1909, he became its Assistant Keeper, and in 1913 he was made the Keeper of the new Sub-Department of Oriental Prints and Drawings.

It was also at this time that he played a crucial role in the formation of Modernism in London by introducing young Imagist poets such as Ezra Pound, Richard Aldington and H.D. (Hilda Doolittle) to East Asian visual art and literature.

Many of Binyon's books produced while at the Museum were influenced by his own sensibilities as a poet, although some are clearly works of plain scholarship, such as his four volume catalogue of all the Museum's English drawings, and his seminal catalogue of Chinese and Japanese prints.

Binyon's poetic reputation before the war, although built on several slim volumes, was such that, on the death of the Poet Laureate Alfred Austin in 1913, Binyon was among the names considered as his likely successor. It was quite a field. Among the other illustrious contenders were Thomas Hardy, John Masefield and Rudyard Kipling; however the post was awarded to Robert Bridges.

Moved and shaken by the onset of the World War I and its military tactics of young men slaughtered to hold or gain a few yards of shell-shocked mud as the British Expeditionary Force began its campaign Binyon wrote his seminal poem For the Fallen, with its Ode of Remembrance (the third and fourth or simply the fourth stanza of the poem). The poem was published by The Times newspaper on September 21st, when public feeling was shaken by the recent Battle of Marne. It became an instant classic, turning moments of great loss into a National and human tribute.

Today, For the Fallen, is often recited at Remembrance Sunday services as well as being an integral part of Anzac Day services in Australia and New Zealand and of November 11th Remembrance Day services in Canada. The "Ode of Remembrance" is now acknowledged as a tribute to all casualties of war, irrespective of nation.

In 1915, despite being too old to enlist, Binyon volunteered at a British hospital for French soldiers, the Hôpital Temporaire d'Arc-en-Barrois, Haute-Marne, France, working for a short time as a hospital orderly.

He returned there in the summer of 1916 and took care of soldiers taken in from the Verdun battlefield. He wrote about his experiences in For Dauntless France (1918) and his poems, "Fetching the Wounded" and "The Distant Guns", were inspired by his hospital service.

After the war, he returned to the British Museum and wrote numerous books on art; especially on William Blake, Persian and Japanese art. His work on ancient Japanese and Chinese cultures offered inspiration that inspired many, among them the poets Ezra Pound and W. B. Yeats. His work on Blake and his followers kept alive the then nearly-forgotten memory of the work of Samuel Palmer. Binyon's spectrum of interests continued the traditional interest of British visionary Romanticism in the rich strangeness of Mediterranean and Oriental cultures.

In 1931, his two volume Collected Poems appeared and by 1932, Binyon was promoted to the post of Keeper of the Prints and Drawings Department. The following year, 1933, he retired from the British Museum. He went to live in the country at Westridge Green, near Streatley but continued writing poetry.

In 1933–1934, Binyon was appointed Norton Professor of Poetry at Harvard University. He delivered a series of lectures on The Spirit of Man in Asian Art, which were published in 1935.

Binyon continued his academic work: in May, 1939 he gave the prestigious Romanes Lecture in Oxford on Art and Freedom, and in 1940 he was appointed the Byron Professor of English Literature at the University of Athens. He worked there until forced to leave by the German invasion of Greece in April, 1941.

Binyon had been friends with Ezra Pound for a long time, and in the 1930s the two became especially close; Pound affectionately called him "BinBin", and he assisted Binyon with his translation of Dante.

Between 1933 and 1943, Binyon published his acclaimed translation of Dante's Divine Comedy in an English version of terza rima, made with some editorial assistance by Ezra Pound. It was acknowledged for many decades as *the* popular translation for Dante readers.

During the horrors of the Second World War Binyon wrote a poem that many claim as to be a masterpiece 'The Burning of the Leaves', puts in print his lines on the London Blitz.

At his death Binyon was working on a major three-part Arthurian trilogy, the first part of which was published after his death as The Madness of Merlin (1947).

Robert Laurence Binyon died in Dunedin Nursing Home, Bath Road, Reading, on March 10th, 1943 after undergoing an operation. A funeral service was held at Trinity College Chapel, Oxford, on March 13th, 1943.

Binyon's ashes were scattered at St. Mary's Church, Aldworth.

On November 11th, 1985, Binyon was among sixteen poets of the Great War commemorated on a slate stone unveiled in Westminster Abbey's Poets' Corner. The inscription on the stone quotes a fellow Great War poet, Wilfred Owen. It reads: "My subject is War, and the pity of War. The Poetry is in the pity."

Laurence Binyon – A Concise Bibliography

Poems and Verse
Persephone (1890)
Lyric Poems (1894)
The Praise of Life (1896)
Porphyrion & Other Poems (1898)
Odes (1901)
Death of Adam & Other Poems (1904)
Penthesilea (1905)
London Visions (1908)
England & Other Poems (1909)
Auguries (1913)
For The Fallen (The Times, September 21st, 1914)
The Winnowing Fan (1914)
The Anvil (1916)
The Cause (1917)
The New World: Poems (1918)

The Secret: Sixty Poems (1920)
The Idols (1928)
Collected Poems Vol I: London Visions, Narrative Poems, Translations (1931)
Collected Poems Vol II: Lyrical Poems (1931)
The North Star & Other Poems (1941)
The Burning of the Leaves & Other Poems (1944)
The Madness of Merlin (1947)

Poems Set to Music

In 1915 Cyril Rootham set "For the Fallen" for chorus and orchestra, first performed in 1919 by the Cambridge University Musical Society conducted by the composer.

Edward Elgar set to music "The Fourth of August", "To Women", and "For the Fallen", as The Spirit of England, Op. 80, for tenor or soprano solo, chorus and orchestra (1917).

English Arts and Myth

Dutch Etchers of the Seventeenth Century (1895), Binyon's first book on painting
John Crone and John Sell Cotman (1897)
William Blake: Being all his Woodcuts Photographically Reproduced in Facsimile (1902)
English Poetry in its relation to painting and the other arts (1918)
Drawings and Engravings of William Blake (1922)
Arthur: A Tragedy (1923)
The Followers of William Blake (1925)
The Engraved Designs of William Blake (1926)
Landscape in English Art and Poetry (1931)
English Watercolours (1933)
Gerard Hopkins and his influence (1939)
Art and freedom. (The Romanes lecture, delivered 25 May 1939). Oxford: The Clarendon press, (1939)

Japanese and Persian Arts

Painting in the Far East (1908)
Japanese Art (1909)
Flight of the Dragon (1911)
The Court Painters of the Grand Moguls (1921)
Japanese Colour Prints (1923)
The Poems of Nizami (1928) (Translation)
Persian Miniature Painting (1933)
The Spirit of Man in Asian Art (1936)
Autobiography[edit]
For Dauntless France (1918) (War memoir)

Biography

Botticelli (1913)
Akbar (1932)

Stage Plays

Brief Candles A verse-drama about the decision of Richard III to dispatch his two nephews

Paris and Œnone. A Tragedy in One Act (1906)

Godstow Nunnery: Play

Boadicea; A Play in eight Scenes

Attila: A Tragedy in Four Acts (1907)

Ayuli: A Play in three Acts and an Epilogue

Sophro the Wise: A Play for Children

(Most of the above were written for John Masefield's theatre).